Bodyweight Training

BY CHRIS COLE

Lose Weight, Build Muscle, Get Lean - The No B.S. Approach to Strength, Conditioning and Bodyweight Training Book

Second Edition

Disclaimer Notice

Please note the information contained within this document is for educational and entertainment purposes only. Every attempt has been made to provide accurate, up to date and reliable complete information. No warranties of any kind are expressed or implied. Readers acknowledge that the author is not engaging in the rendering of legal, financial, medical or professional advice.

By reading this document, the reader agrees that under no circumstances are we responsible for any losses, direct or indirect, which are incurred as a result of the use of information contained within this document, including, but not limited to, — errors, omissions, or inaccuracies.

Table Contents

Introduction

Welcome to the complete guide to making your body stronger, better and worth looking at. As the title suggests, this eBook will cover all the smart methods that will help you gain fitness in your life. 'Might is right' may not be the mantra of life anymore, but strength cannot be completely ruled out as an essential part of our lives. Some people are fitness freaks and choose to exercise on a routine, while others hit the local gym to build a toned body.

Your body is a temple and you are the God sitting inside it. You deserve to be worshiped and attended to. This eBook will cover all the 'offerings' and 'sacrifices' you must make in order to take care of this holy temple. Do not ignore the need of your muscles to stretch and gain some strength. You will be walked through everything, step by step, that needs to be followed and adapted to help you gain the required stamina to advance through the prescribed exercises.

I hope you get the most out of this eBook so let's begin our journey towards your increased fitness and a toned body!

Chapter 1

Why Should You Focus On Strength Building?

Welcome to the first chapter of this book which has been designed to make you aware of the amazing benefits of bodyweight training. First let me begin by telling you why bodyweight training is so effective.

So Why Bodyweight Training

To answer that I have a list of a few good reasons, beginning with this. Bodyweight training exercises have been proven to give amazingly high fitness growth in a very short times. As there is no need to set up, calibrate and strap yourself into one fitness machine – after extracting yourself from another – you can move straight from one exercise to another in a few seconds without stopping to rest.

You can mix up cardiovascular and muscle building training by changing from performing burpees for cardio then moving onto press ups for muscle. This keeps your heart rate up throughout all the exercises you do while allowing your muscles to grow.

This in turn leads to another good reason for bodyweight training – it burns fat very efficiently. Even just a brief session of bodyweight training has a massive influence on your body's metabolism and this elevated state can last for hours even after your workout is finished.

Regardless of your current fitness level, bodyweight training is a challenge. Especially for a beginner, but even those who have been training in gyms for years. Just by adding a few extra repetitions, performing the exercises really fast or at half the normal speed or adding in a clap at the top of a press up can all have a massive impact on the intensity and difficulty of the work out. Plus every time you make a change, the benefits and growth are evident.

It improves your core strength. It takes nearly thirty different muscles to make up your core, not just the famous 'abs' and bodyweight training exercises can make use of them all at the same time. You will get better abdominal muscles but also get better posture, be less likely to suffer from lower back pain and generally improve your techniques.

It is better for your joints than other forms of exercise. Many people who train in gyms also suffer from joint problems and stiff muscles. Bodyweight training helps eliminate this by using a full range of motions making sure your joints remain flexible and moving freely. This in turn can help to improve your posture and limit the possibility of injury through exercising.

You never have an excuse to avoid working out. As there is no need for expensive gym memberships or the setup of a complete home gym, bodyweight exercises give an advantage over these. In addition, many people cite they do not have enough time, are too busy or it is too inconvenient to do a workout but the versatility of bodyweight training means you can do it wherever you are, at whatever time.

You can get much better balance. Because exercises like squats and one legged squats involve moving your whole body up and down in an upright position, they improve balance due to your greater awareness of your body and the control you get as your muscles begin to build.

So for these and many other reasons, bodyweight training is a versatile and worthwhile form of exercise for anyone.

Simply put, as humans we are genetically predisposed to benefit from this type of training. Look at the animal kingdom – we are animals after all – how many overweight animals do you see in the wild? I bet the answer is none. Many people will tell you this is because there is not enough food for them, another answer is that they only eat when they are hungry and use their muscles to get it. We have developed to such an extent we no longer have to hunt our meat or gather our plants, we can have it delivered directly to our doors now.

The fact is that most humans pale in comparison to most wild animals and we are so far removed from what nature – or God – intended it is ridiculous. Chimps and gorillas, for example, never spend their time pumping weights endlessly in a gym, never spend thousands on expensive exercise equipment – how many bananas would you need to buy a treadmill anyway – so how is it they are virtually all at their physical peaks? Natural bodyweight training. Using their bodies to climb, run, jump and play fight, as nature – or God – intended. So if it works for other animals, why not for humans? The simple answer is, it will.

The word ‘strength’ has been used in a very literal way in this eBook. It refers to physical brute or raw muscles that provide you with the kinetic energy to carry out all the basic works in your lives that require labor. Strength building has its own benefits. Let us look at some of them briefly.

When you are beefed up, you come across as a strong, confident man. You not only inspire safety among your companions but you can also use your strength to your own advantage in unforeseen circumstances. Imagine going out with a group of your friends to a party and coming across a bunch of good for nothings who try to rob you of your valuables. Your strength is your only resort. Words and wit work only in books and courtrooms; everywhere else, it's the use of strength that saves the day.

Strength builds your body, gives it a shape and tones you up for a healthy life. The gains that are extracted from having a toned body are numerous but most of them help you move faster towards a better and healthier life. It has been shown by various studies worldwide that a stronger person, who is in regular shape, has longer life expectancy than a person who is either frail or obese. Not to mention, obesity has its own set of complications later in life. It is always advisable to choose a fit body over any other option.

A good body is a good way to strengthen your mental faculties. The phrase 'mental faculties' includes self-confidence, self-esteem and overall readiness of your mind. There are many situations in life that you refrain from venturing into only because your body is not fit for it. From trying out tight fitting clothes to exploring a new area of adventurous sport, it all includes a fit body.

You are naturally likely to gain self-confidence when your body is in the right shape and size. Your body's shape is connected to your mental functioning in unimaginable ways. You may not realize it but when your body is shaped in the appropriate way, you assume confidence like no one else. The effect a good body has on those around you is also exceptional. A good-looking body is always the center of attraction of a crowd. You may not be verbally rich but you can make up for that using some simple ways to gain strength and eventually a nicely toned body.

Everybody has a certain social worth attached to his name. People with intellect, people with money and people with a good body are all looked up to and respected in society. Out of these three, money, body and intellect, if you lack in one, you can always make up for it with the other two. Let us focus on the third essential, which is the body. Say you have not been blessed with the gift of the gab and you aren't so economically enriched either. Now the only department that remains is physique. You can always work on this field, as it's the only one besides money that can be cultivated and earned and for free. Intellect is always good for the mind, but exercise is good for the body and the mind. You may be good with words but when you enter the practical arena, a good body always scores over everything else.

Your social worth definitely takes a flight upwards when you are a toned person. The first impressions attached to your presence in a group will more than enough to socially launch you into good and desirable company. Coming to the point I have been subtly trying to make, your chances of finding a romantic partner increases greatly when you are physically toned. If you are a guy in his twenties, you will gain a lot from a good body in the love department. Love cannot be manufactured, or bought, but working towards a great body can double the opportunities you get.

Strength building involves a series of processes, such a series brings routine and punctuality to your life. Therefore you not only work for a better body, but also manage your daily schedule in such a way that your gym time does not get interrupted. This will eventually become a habit which will cross over into other areas of your life and you will realize you are slowly starting to get far more disciplined in life.

In a nutshell, strength building is desirable for anybody who wants to enhance their social, mental and physical worth. Remember, it is not for others that you are indulging in strength building activities; it is for your own well-being and survival in the end. Nature has always exercised it's 'Survival of the Fittest' policy in this one way or another so where is the problem with giving yourself the advantage of being one *of* the fittest? In spite of how advanced and civilized we have become, it often comes down to brute strength at the end of the day. The stronger you are, the better your chances of survival. After all, Charles Darwin did leave us with a perfect solution for survival - Strength.

Chapter 2
How to Build Strength?

Welcome to the second chapter of the guide to fitness and a healthier life. Without beating around the bush much, we'll get straight down to business.

The first step of any journey is setting of goals. Without a specific aim in mind, you are likely to fail in any adventure you embark on. Hence, the first hurdle that you have to cross is a good and achievable aim. Set your ambitions wisely. If you are under-estimating yourself, you will most likely set easy goals. On the other hand, you run the risk of setting really high goals if you are under the influence of self-overestimation. Adopt a realistic approach in this step, as it is vital for the future of your health journey. Remember, you are choosing to go on a journey – without having first made certain what your destination is, you will be heading out without a direction.

Set your goals on a daily, weekly, monthly or yearly basis, it often helps to write them down and leave them somewhere you can see them often – on a fridge or your front door – then make sure you look at them. How you set your goals depends largely upon how long you want to continue your workout regimes, but it is advisable to opt for the longer-term, since it will benefit you in a wholesome way. As with dieting, strength training and fitness depends upon continuing with some form of the activity. If you stick to a diet only long enough to lose the weight you want, then eat normally, the weight would pile back on. Similarly with strength training, if you stop once you have reached your goal, your body will lose tone and return to the state it was in before you began. Make sure you bear this in mind when planning and setting your goals.

After having set a goal, it is time for you to start taking baby steps. Start out by first establishing your den. Your den could be your home where you have installed some basic equipment for working out, or it could also be the local gym that has got the option of hiring a personal trainer. Subscribe to such a gym arena and start your journey on a mild note.

Make a workout plan. A workout plan must be meticulously designed and efficiently timed. It serves no purpose for you to pile up every exercise under the sun into your workout plan and expect to follow it through with implementation. Consult a personal trainer if you have to and sit down and plot your workout schedules.

Choose a light exercise to begin with. The part of any workout plan that prepares you for the main sweating is known as warming up. You achieve half the result in this stage itself. This stage decides whether you are going to make it or break it. The idea behind performing warm-ups before rigorous exercises is to prevent your body from suffering from long lasting injuries and pain. Let us have a look at some of the most commonly followed warm-up exercises.

Marching

Assume a straight position and march on the spot. You cannot move forward you have to march while remaining on the same spot. Keep your fists gentle and loose while doing this since it's a light routine. Make sure your arms are in synchronization with your legs. A leg down and then a leg up is the right way to go about doing this.

Heel digs

Stand on a spot and extend your right leg forward. Use your left leg to provide support to the rest of your body. Extend both your arms forward at the same time as your right leg. Now repeat the procedure with the left leg, moving forward the second time.

Knee Lifts

This is the funniest warm up exercise ever invented. Stand tall and lift your left leg until your heel touches your right knee. Now place your right palm over the left leg's knee. You are now in a Hindu goddess position. Stay in this posture for about 20 seconds and switch to the right leg to repeat the same process.

Shoulder rolls

Perhaps the most liberating and fun part of your warming up regime, shoulder rolls are supposed to be done while you are standing still. Of late, however, a recent development has made sure you get added benefits from doing a mixture of marching and shoulder rolls. For this, you have to march on the spot for five rounds, stand still and switch to doing shoulder rolls for the next five rounds. Alternate both the techniques to get awesome benefits.

Knee bends

Stand in a half bent position with your arms outstretched and parallel to the ground. Drop a little towards the ground, thereby giving the impression of a half a squat. Get back to your original position quickly and repeat the process.

Chapter 3

What Are Bodyweight Training and Calisthenics?

Calisthenics and bodyweight training are basically the same thing, bodyweight training used to be known as calisthenics, but the name is now making a huge comeback as more and more athletes start to incorporate it into their daily training routine. Calisthenics is one of the most unique sports in the world because there is no requirement for expensive equipment, expensive gym passes or any real education to do it. Calisthenics can be done anywhere, at any time and the only limit to it is your imagination!

As with anything, there are plenty of advantages and there are also plenty of misconceptions to bodyweight training. In a physical sense, it is one of the most beneficial sports there is. Where weight lifting may affect your joints, bodyweight training is completely safe. In fact, the very act of stretching your skeleton out properly with exercises like pull-ups can help to improve your posture and get rid of any niggling back issues you may be suffering from.

Calisthenics has also been shown to improve your stamina, energy, strength and agility as well as your balance and coordination while promoting overall health and fitness. It can also help to improve your mental health and relieve stress, depression and anxiety as well as giving you back your self-esteem.

One of the biggest misconceptions about bodyweight training is that only people with thinner bones can do it. The opposite is in fact true, anyone can do this, no matter what age or size you are. It may interest you to know that the current world record holder for pull-ups is an 85 kg Russian man and, back in the 1930's, Strongman Bert Assirati, weighing in at 120 kg, was perhaps the heaviest person to ever perform the iron cross and could do a one armed handstand with ease.

Another misconception is that you cannot use bodyweight training to gain muscle. Again, the opposite is true, you can by simply altering the exercise to make it harder and giving yourself a leverage disadvantage. However, you do run the risk of injury and strains if you are not careful or are not experienced.

The Ten Commandments of Calisthenics for Big Muscles

Athletes, whether old or young, are moving over to bodyweight training in their hundreds. In fact, bodyweight training is the new black! It seems that people are finally realizing that this is the way to go to get a fully functioning, supple, coordinated and balanced body, abandoning gyms and their fancy equipment in their droves. However, while bodyweight training is the in thing right now, many athletes and coaches still haven't grasped just how awesome it really can be for building up muscle mass.

It's all about using bodyweight exercises in a specific way to develop your movement skills and strength while keeping your body mass at a lean level to keep yourself looking sleek and lithe if you don't want to be carrying around extra pounds with huge muscles. If you do want those bulging muscles, you simply change your game plan again. The following list of Ten Commandments are essential for those of you who want to use bodyweight training to bulge out the muscles while retaining your suppleness and keeping your joints safe from injury.

Commandment 1 – Embrace those reps

The current trend these days in training is low reps, low fatigue and high sets. This is a great way to build up your skill levels in specific movements and it works by training your nervous system to build muscle memory. To do this, you need to repeat an exercise a number of times to perfect it, to train your brain into not knowing what the optimal movement sequence is and you do this by performing low reps. Nothing hard, nothing long that will burn your energy up quickly. Rest up and try again. This is how the low bodyweight, lean athletes train to build up their strength without building up the muscle mass. If you want the muscle mass, increase the reps to a higher volume.

The reason for this is because you first need to become weak in order to become bigger and stronger. Big muscles are developed by draining your muscle cells of chemical energy. As time goes by, your body will respond to this by producing more chemical energy in your muscle cells. This, in turn makes them swell up, giving you those big muscles you always dreamed of. But in order to get your body to produce this energy and increase your storage level, you have to get rid of what is already there. In a big way. Low intensity exercise simply won't work because energy will simply be used up from fatty acids instead of from muscle cells. Alternating reps and rests will not cut it either because chemical energy regenerates very quickly and will never get low enough for your body to have to produce more and store it. You need to tough it out, grit your teeth and push out continuous high intensity reps. Forget singles, doubles and triples, start looking at a minimum of five reps, preferably a lot more.

Commandment 2 – Work Hard

An easy way to train is to do low intensity reps, keep yourself fresh and rest between each set. But, if you want to really work yourself, you need to push yourself, go through rep after continuous rep of hard exercises. This makes it much tougher and the more reps you do, the harder it is going to get. This is when your muscles start burning and crying out for mercy. The burning sensation is the chemical energy being used up as fuel and that is what you want! Your heart rate should increase, you will be covered with sweat, trembling and your whole system will feel stressed out. You might even feel a little nauseous and that is exactly what you want.

Commandment 3 – Compound, simple exercises are the way to go

Following on from the previous two, if you are going to push yourself to your limit, you must avoid complex exercises that require a lot of skill. Exercises like handstands would cause your form to collapse before you could push hard enough to exhaust the energy from your muscles. If these are the type of exercise you prefer, stick to low fatigue, low reps, and high sets. To build up that muscle you need to use simple exercises.

Do not mistake simple for easy though – a simple exercise is a one armed push up, twenty times in a row and that isn't easy!

Stick to doing exercises that you can put a whole bundle of muscular energy into without using up nervous energy on your balance, gravity, coordination and body placement. Try to use dynamic exercises, those that you go up and down in, like pushups, pull-ups, etc., as these are far better than static holds and drain the chemical energy much better and faster at the same time as requiring less concentration.

The absolute best dynamic exercises are compound ones, using several muscle groups at the same time. Try to focus on the following exercises:

- Pull-ups
- Pistol squats
- Bodyweight squats
- Shrimp squats
- Push ups
- Australian variants of pull-ups
- Bridges
- Dips

- Handstand pushups – do these against a wall, as they require more effort!
- Leg raises

Don't exclude skill-based exercises, like elbow levers, from your regime, but don't rely on them to build up your muscle mass, it won't happen.

Commandment 4 – Limit your sets

If you are doing this right, if you are doing the hard exercises and putting all your effort into sufficient reps to completely exhaust your muscles, you do not need to perform a lot of sets. In order to trigger the mechanism that calls on your body to add more storage capacity for chemical energy, you need to push your body and deplete cells beyond anything you are comfortable with. Once you reach that point and that mechanism is triggered, why do you need to keep on triggering it? All you are doing is wasting time and energy and causing damage to your muscles which is not necessary. It also eats up the time you would be using for recovery.

"You can take a stick of dynamite and tap it with a pencil all day and it's not going to go off. But hit it once with a hammer and 'BANG'—it will go off!" – Mike Mentzer

The biological switch that you need to flick to trigger off muscle growth needs to be hammered not flicked with a pencil. One set, one hard, exhaustive set of compound exercises is worth way more than 20 or 30 reps of a halfhearted attempt. Aim for two hard sets for each exercise, after you have warmed up properly. You can grow those muscles with one set but two will ensure you get the results you want. If you are new to this, do a few more sets, just to build up your experience with a particular movement – practice, in a nutshell.

Adding more sets to your program does not equate to hard, high performance training. Instead, it promotes the opposite. More than two sets will cause one of two things to happen – you will give all you have and your last few sets will be somewhat pathetic, or you will pace yourself out which means your sets are weaker and not having the desired effect. Neither will have given you the muscle growth you are looking for; all they will do is hinder your recovery and could even cause injury. Training hard is far better than training long. Short and sharp will win the race any day of the week!

Commandment 5 – Focus on your progress and use a journal to track training

You may find this hard to believe but there are people who follow the first four commandments to the letter and still can't get the results. Why? Is it in their makeup? Are they training without the use of steroids? Perhaps their gym doesn't sell the latest high toxicity supplements? In fact, it's none of these. It's because they don't keep a track of their progress, which means they have nothing to work towards.

When you train, your body will adapt to the stress but only a little. You might make small improvements, maybe add in another rep, improve your form a little and your recovery time is increased somewhere else. Over a long period of time, these improvements begin to add up, showing you how some of these athletes seem to be able to double, even triple their strength, add on inches of muscle and make themselves into a being that is superior.

Unfortunately, many athletes don't take any notice of these small improvements and never build on them, as they should. These changes are what are known as a window of opportunity, and so many people ignore them. If you could increase your strength by 1% a week, you would double your strength, maybe more, in just 2 years. Most athletes don't accurately track their progress and, because of this, they never spot the windows of opportunity that present themselves.

1% is, in reality, a tiny target to aim for. Trying to use your memory or instinct to hit the spot won't work and this is why many trainee athletes fail – they struggle to see or remember the target clearly. Using a journal to log your progress makes the target clear and quantifiable. Athletes who use a log to chart their workouts and the results find that, all of a sudden, they know exactly what to aim for with every single workout and they never miss that tiny target.

While the first four commandments are valuable ones, without pulling them all together to harness them, they are next to useless. You have to track your progress, daily, weekly, monthly and yearly. It really doesn't matter if the improvement is small or seems to be insignificant – it is a progress and it must be charted. Over time, small and regular improvements equal a larger one. In short, the real secret to big muscles and strength gain without the use of drugs is to focus on the small improvements and continue to build on them.

Training journals are vital if your goal is muscle building. So many athletes will flood their bodies with supplements that are effectively worthless but they won't take five minutes to fill out a training log. This is quite ironic because those five minutes are worth more and will do more for your physique than any supplement in the world. Not only are journals vital for progress, they are also helpful in mastering the science of training, giving yourself feedback and improving mindfulness when you work out and much more besides.

Commandment 6 – Rest is vital for growth

Following on from the concept of progress comes rest or training frequency. Before you argue that you have to keep going to build those muscles, ask yourself one question – if you want to improve on your last session add in one more rep, or tighten your form up, how do you do it? Do you want to be tired out, beaten up and weary? Of course you don't, that would be plain stupid!

You want to be well rested, refreshed enough to hammer your workout into the ground, break your own personal records, improve on your best times and increase your reps. Let me give you the perfect example of rest – Sir Roger Bannister rested up for five days before he broke the record for the four minute mile.

Unfortunately, many trainees do not rest anywhere near as much as they should. They read too many muscle magazines, following the stories of and trying to copy the workout routines of people who are stuffed full of steroids – people who can train all day long if they want but get nowhere. The reason they are getting nowhere is because they are tired – their bodies and their minds. Their muscles are not being given the opportunity to repair and rest, let alone recover and increase in size. Their muscles are torn down and weak not big, strong and healthy. These people forget one golden rule of training and muscle building – you grow when you rest, not when you are working out. How much rest you need depends on a number of factors, such as your age, training experience, constitution, what other activities you do etc. So, while I can't tell you how much to rest, I can give you some general pointers:

- If you want to gain muscle size, never work the same muscle more than twice in a week
- It really doesn't matter how often you train, it's how much progress you make that counts
- Some of the biggest musclemen in the world train for just three days a week but they train hard. It is a huge misconception that you need to train every single day for hours
- Working one muscle hard once a week and showing progress is worth far more than working it three or four times a week and moving backwards rather than forwards.
- You should never train any muscle two days running, not when you are doing hard exercise
- Bigger muscles need more time to recover than smaller ones
- If a muscle group is sore, avoid training it

- As well as chemical energy from the muscle cells, muscle training will also deplete your energy and hormone systems. If you begin to feel low, tire or experience a real lack of energy, add in more rest days to your program
- Always rest for at least two days every week if you want the maximum gains, unless your workouts are low impact. Even then, you should aim for three to four days off from your program every week

The bottom line is this – to build muscles you need to improve continuously by pushing harder over less sets. To do this, you need to properly rest your body, mind and muscles. Rest is probably a larger piece of the workout puzzle than many people realize and that is why they never completely achieve their full potential.

Commandment 7 – Stop eating clean all the time

Now we come to nutrition. You read all the time about how you should eat clean whole foods all the time. How many times have you read an article that tells you to eat broccoli and chicken breast with none of that lovely juicy skin on it? Or steamed fish and spinach! And let's not forget all those lovely supplements you are told to take, washed down with several liters of water!

While it is important to eat properly, it will not kill you to eat a bit of junk food every now and again. Junk food actually has an anabolic effect on the body and many athletes looking to build muscle will bite your hand off to get a bit of junk into their bodies – simply because they are fully aware of the growth potential it holds. In fact, this kind of food has a better effect on the muscular body than steroid drugs, which are considered a big no-no these days and are really not required.

Obviously if you are on a weight loss regime rather than muscle building you won't be filling up on junk food and, to be fair, most bodybuilders don't fill up on the stuff; they simply eat it when they want to without worrying about the effect. Look at it this way – many diets preclude the use of quick acting carbohydrates because carbs are seen as the bad guy. But, the people who follow these diets are also quite happy to take quick acting protein powders. The human body's primary source of fuel is carbohydrate and the quicker acting they are, the better. Fast protein does not have the same effect in this case and is probably nothing more than useless.

And let's not forget the fat. Stop steering clear of proper muscle foods like cheese, eggs, sausage and red meat. Stop wasting money on amino acids and whey shakes when they simply don't work and eat a proper meal instead! Testosterone is the muscle-building hormone in the body and that is synthesized from cholesterol in your body. If you don't eat enough of the right high fat foods, your body doesn't get the level of cholesterol it needs and it can't make the testosterone. That means no muscles.

Vegans spend all their time moaning about the amount of pathogens in meat but recent studies have shown that, rather than being responsible for early deaths, red meat may actually be what is responsible for the abnormally long life of the human race. Think about it – our ancestors lived on slabs of meat and they had nowhere near the illnesses that today's world does.

So, I'm not saying you should dive into a diet of junk food but a little every now and again really won't hurt you. To grow those muscles, eat a healthy balanced diet but keep in mind that you do not have to eat clean all the time. Throw a candy bar into the mix occasionally and enjoy it without guilt.

Commandment 8 – Get plenty of sleep

One thing that many people focus on in the world of muscle building and body conditioning is prison athletes. How do they get such dense muscle and how do they keep it when those who are filling their bodies full of supplements remain skinny and mouse-like in comparison? There are lots of reasons for this. First is routine in work and eating, then there's the motivation of training hard; there are no distractions in prison ether but there is a much bigger reason – sleep. When you sleep, your brain doesn't, it continues to work and one of the things it does is sends an order to your body to produce performance enhancing drugs – natural ones.

Prison inmates sleep better than anyone does, simply because they have little choice when the lights are turned out. And, there is the matter of routine – their bodies are conditioned to accept that when the lights go out at a specific time, their bodies and minds shut down as well. It's the same time every day, without fail. And this is how our ancestors lived as well. In their case, lights out was sun down, the time when the brain and body switch off to recharge. Many prison inmates get at least 10 hours sleep a night and a few naps throughout the day as well.

Outside of prison, things are different and this is why we struggle to reap the same results. We control our own artificial sunlight with lights, phones, laptops and other means. We can sit up and watch TV all night if we want or go out and party until the sun comes up. As a result of this, our sleeping patterns are in total chaos, especially in the younger generation. We suffer more interrupted sleep and insomnia than ever before and our brains are so muddled that, half the time, it's a wonder we can even function. Routine doesn't exist and we do not get enough sleep to function.

Many fitness magazines tend to put rest and sleep in the same category and they couldn't be further apart. A ten-minute rest does not, in any way, provide the same benefits as ten, twenty or even sixty minutes of sleep. Sleep does what rest cannot do but you can't turn that around – rest doesn't play the same role. Rest is good, is necessary for your body to repair but sleep is unique in what it can do. When you sleep:

- Your brain will produce GH – growth hormone - which is healthy and free when you sleep but illegal and dangerous, not to mention expensive when bought on the streets.

- Your brain also generates natural melatonin, which is one of the most powerful healing and immunity compounds known to the scientific world. High levels of melatonin help muscles to heal and can even help to keep cancer at bay.

- Your brain also produces LH – luteinizing hormone – which stimulates interstitial cells in the testicles to produce that all-important testosterone.

And that really is just for starters! Sleep is vital to the growth of muscles and if that doesn't push you into making sure you get enough, bear this in mind – extra sleep has been proven to make you ripped!

Your sleep-wake cycle also regulates your eating patterns, something that not too many people understand. Back when humankind was beginning to evolve, late summer was when the fruiting season began, when the days were longer. Our ancestors would stuff themselves with carb laden fruits in a bid to stock up on stores of body fat for the long winter ahead. These days we prolong our daylight hours artificially, fooling our brains into believing it is permanently late summer. Because of this, our brains churn out neurotransmitters and hormones that are designed to make us eat as much carb laden foods as we can find – mostly the wrong sort. This is why most people fail at diets – our bodies are permanently trying to stock up for winter.

The answer is to go to bed early, get your body conditioned to lights out at a certain time and your internal body clock won't be fooled into thinking its fruit season all year round. Try it and you will suddenly find that you are not craving high carb foods all the time. Something else that sleep does is cause leptin to be produced by your fat cells. Leptin is otherwise known as the "lean hormone" and it promotes a sudden release of energy from fatty tissues in the body this in turn inhibits hunger.

Commandment 9 – Train your mind, not just your body

This is so true. Too many people concentrate on what their bodies look like and forget about their brains. The mind has a fundamental role in training and so many people miss it because their focus is elsewhere. The mind is more powerful than the most powerful of supplements ever produced, including food supplements. The human mind will always take you in the right direction if you just stop long enough to listen to it. The only time it won't is when negative influences hold it back. These negative influences are thought patterns that are damaging and destructive ideas. In order to achieve your full potential, you must train yourself to listen to your mind and not to all the rubbish that is printed in so called health and fitness magazines – you know the ones, those that contain numerous ads for the next greatest product to help you build muscle and lose weight.

You also need to think about your body in a positive way. This means taking any negative thoughts and feelings and getting rid of them completely. If you hate the way your body looks or works and simply concentrate on the negative, your results will be far smaller and the effort you put in will be wasted. Look at it this way, you meet someone you went to school with a few years after leaving. They see you and try to ignore you but you decide to be the bigger person and go over to talk to them.

"Hi, Brian, how're things going?" You ask in your polite way.

"Oh, it's you," Brian moans, "Things are fine I suppose."

"What are you up to now?" You wonder.

"Well, I pretty much run things around here, you know," Brian explains, "What about you? Are you still broke and clutching at straws to get by? What about that girl you were with? You know, the ugly one with a big nose?" Brian doesn't even wait for an answer before going on, "Still, glad you're here, is there any chance you could help me move some furniture this weekend?"

I think your answer is likely to be "NO!" and you would be right to say so. However, this is how your body feels when you think badly about it. You hate your legs, your bum is saggy, etc. So why would you expect to get the best results from something you think about in a detrimental way?

Try and concentrate on the positive aspects, someone with even the lowest self esteem must be able to say they have a pair of eyes which see the world clearly, or a pair of legs they rely on to get around. Even if your legs don't work and you need a wheelchair to get about, try and think about a different part of you. You have a pair of strong arms which move your chair and help you get around, you have two excellent ears which allow you to hear the world around you. And great hair.

Commandment 10 – Get strong

Strength is gained by proper training of your nervous system and mass is built by training your muscles. The previous nine commandments showed you some of the most powerful ways to train your muscles but please don't think I am telling you to ignore strength training if you want bigger muscles.

The nervous system and the muscular system have a complex relationship. Think of them as the nervous system being an electrical circuit and the muscles being a light bulb. The higher the wattage on the electrical circuit, the brighter that bulb will burn. In the same way, the more you push your nervous system, the harder your muscles are going to contract and the stronger you will be. Bodybuilders train their muscles while strength athletes concentrate on their nervous system. You don't need bigger bulbs when you can get smaller but more powerful ones!

Both types of athlete are looking for more light out of their bulb, which, in your terms, means they want more out of their muscles. Athletes who want more from their muscles go for bigger bulbs – they increase their mass as well as their strength. At the opposite end of the scale, the bodybuilder wants lighter or more muscular output capacity because it lets them lift more and do harder exercises. Let's face it, the bigger a body builder is, the more weight they have to lift to keep on making progress.

What I am trying to say is, if you want muscle gain, you need to train your nervous system as well as your muscles. Get strong and release your full potential.

Chapter 4

Exercises for Every Part of You

Ones Which Do It All

To begin with, here are a few exercises which strengthen, tone and build muscle when performed in conjunction with the advice above. Never forget the all-important warm-up exercises which get your heart beating, your lungs working and your whole body ready for these workouts.

Some of the exercises below are suitable for anyone from complete amateurs, while some might need a little working up to – I'm thinking of the handstand press up here – and the help of a friend the first few times. Just remember, the more of these things you do, the better you will get, the more muscle you will gain and the fitter you will be.

Okay, here goes.

Exercises for the whole body

The Inchworm

Standing up straight with your feet slightly apart, bend slowly forward until your hands are on the floor. Keeping your legs straight – without locking the knees – make your hands walk forwards until you reach a press up position. From there, take small steps with your feet until your toes touch your wrists, then walk your hands forward again. Just like an inchworm – hence the name, clever eh? - you might find this exercise needs a little more room than you have and need to turn around as, unlike an inchworm, you cannot crawl up the wall. Five or six repetitions of this should get you across the living room.

Bear Crawl

Drop down onto your hands and knees then tighten your abdominal muscles to raise you up onto your tiptoes. Keeping your balance, move your right arm and knee forwards as far as possible, then repeat with your left arm and knee. Repeat these actions about ten times but don't rifle through the rubbish bins – you're meant to be eating healthily.

Tuck Jump

Well this one is self-explanatory really, so I'll explain it anyway. Stand with your knees bent a little then jump as high as you can. Following on with the jumping action, while in the air, pull your knees up to your chest and thrust out your arms. Initially you might need to put your arms out sideways for balance but with practice you'll be able to throw them forwards as well. Uncurl your body and land lightly – hopefully – on your feet, bending slightly before leaping up into the next jump.

The Mountain Climb

On hands and knees again, tuck your left knee up to your chest and extend your right leg backwards. From this position and keeping your hands on the floor, jump up and switch legs so you end up with your right foot underneath your chest and with your left leg stretched out behind you. Repeat five or six times until you're ready to tackle K2

Press up (With added extra)

Try this on a soft surface if you can, padding is definitely recommended. Start off with a normal press up – hands flat on the floor, back straight, on your toes – drop to the floor then push upwards. That added extra comes now, you need to jump up with your arms. Yes, you're reading this right, jump your hands up off the floor then land, do the press up and jump again. You shouldn't expect to get three or four feet off the ground, but as long as you get your hands off the floor, you're doing well and you can work up to the higher jumps as your strength and muscles grow.

Climb the Stairs and Curl Your Biceps

Pretty simple this one, rather than spending money on Stairmasters, use some real stairs! Walk up and down your chosen set of stairs for a muscle building, cardiovascular workout. Add in some biceps curls, with bottles of water as free weights, for a full-body workout.

Walkout

Similar in style to the Inchworm, get on all fours and walk your hands forward but keep your toes where they are. Once you reach a press up position, walk your hands back towards the start position. Rinse and repeat (without the rinse)

The Burpee (It had to be in here somewhere)

Probably one of the best full-body workout exercises ever thought of. Begin in a squatting position with your hands flat on the floor. Kick both your feet out backwards to assume a press up start position, do one press up and then bring your feet back up so you end up in the squatted, start position.

The Plank

Lying face down with your forearms on the floor and your shoulders at right angles. With your legs straight out behind, supported on your toes. Lift your body off the floor so your whole body rests on your toes and forearms. This will put strain in your core muscles and you should aim to hold the position for as long as possible before relaxing and repeating. If you can hold this position for a minute you're doing well – just remember to breathe.

The Plank Into The Press Up

Starting in the plank position above, bring first one, then the other arm into a press up position before bringing them back into the plank position again. Make sure to alternate the arm you begin this exercise with each time you perform it. Change things up a little by actually doing the press up before going back to the plank position again.

Exercises for the Legs

The Wall Sit

Not as easy as it might sound, with your back against a wall – making sure it's sturdy – lower yourself down the wall until you're in a sitting position. With your thighs parallel to the floor and your knees above your ankles, keep your back straight and flat against the wall, holding the position for a minute before returning to the standing, start position.

Lunges

Put your hands on your hips with your feet hip width apart then move one leg forwards, lowering your body until the front leg is bent at least a right angle – go far enough for your knee to touch the floor if you can – and your other leg is stretched out behind you. Slowly lift yourself back up until in the start position again and repeat with the other leg moving forward. Change things up a bit by stepping your leg backwards into the lunge.

Lunge Into Row

Perform a lunge as described above, then once you have your balance back, bring up the leg you stepped forward with and then lift it until at right angles and lift both hands above your head. Grab those bottles of water as weights for some added intensity.

Pistol Squats

A really intense exercise this one, begin with your arms out in front of you, then bring up your right leg until it's at right angles with your body. Then lower your whole body into a one-legged squat – holding this position if you can – before pushing back up and lowering your right leg. Repeat the whole sequence with your left leg. Intensify this workout by wrapping a piece of rope around a sturdy pole and leaning back. Hold the rope so your body is at a forty five degree angle then do the squat. Bear in mind you are using your entire bodyweight to work *one* of your legs! Who says you can't gain muscle through bodyweight training?

Lunge Jumps

You'll need good balance for this one! Begin with a normal lunge as described above but once you have dropped down into the lunge, jump up, using your arms for thrust and balance, and switch leg position to land in the lunge position with the leg you had at the front now behind you. Can you do ten of these?

Curtsey Lunge

On the off chance you end up in the presence of royalty, you can still do some bodyweight training. Once down in the lunge position, with your right leg out in front, bring your left leg around behind the right at an angle. Lower your hips and bend your knees until your right leg is almost parallel to the floor. Make sure you keep your body upright and your hips squared.

Squats

With hands on hips, stand with your feet parallel and slightly spread apart. Bend your knees and hips until you are crouched down and your thighs are parallel to the ground. Your heels should stay flat on the floor as you do this, don't go up on tiptoe, then lift yourself back up to the starting position.

Squat Jump With Reach

To add some cardiovascular exercise to a normal squat, add a jump in just for fun. Once down in the normal squat, jump in the air and thrust your arms above your head before landing again and dropping down into the squat again. If you really want to make this exercise a powerful one, combine it with the tuck jump described above.

One Legged Dead Lift

Begin by standing straight up with both feet together then lift your right leg a little. Bending at the waist, let your arms and torso move forward while extending your right leg out behind you for balance. Lean over as far as you can, almost touching the floor with your hands before slowly pulling back to the start position and changing legs.

Squat Into Seated Pose

Beginning with your feet hip distance apart and standing upright, drop down into a squat until your thighs sit level with the floor. Bring your arms up then straighten your legs, raising your right leg and bringing your left arm across as far as possible. Go back to the start position and repeat but raise your left leg this time.

Quadruped Leg Lifts

Begin on hands and knees, with a straight back and your abdominal muscles clenched. Lift your right leg and extend it straight back out behind you, pointing your toes. Once you gain your balance, lift the toes of your left leg so you are balanced on two hands and one knee only, tighten your abdominal and gluteus muscles, hold for ten to fifteen seconds and swap to the other leg.

Step Ups

Maybe this one is too obvious to describe but... Stand before your chosen step, stair or bench, put your right foot up on the surface and step up until your leg is fully straight. Step back down and put your foot back on the floor. Repeat for ten or twelve turns per side.

Tiptoe Raises

As it sounds, this exercise has you starting with your feet flat on the floor. Raise your whole body up, lifting your heels and moving onto your toes. Hold for a few seconds then relax. In order to add extra range to this exercise, stand with your heels hanging over the edge and when you lower yourself back down, drop your heels below the level of the step.

Chest and Back Exercises

Press Ups

Just about the most famous bodyweight training exercise ever, begin with your hands about shoulder width apart and your legs out straight. Lower your torso down to the floor and push it back up again. This movement is most effective when you keep your elbows pulled tightly in to the sides of your body as you make it.

Press Up From Dolphin

You don't need to find an actual dolphin for this, luckily, as the name comes from the original start position – a yoga position called the dolphin – similar to downward dog but with your elbows on the floor. So elbows on floor, back arched to make an inverted V shape, with your bottom pointing up at the ceiling, and feet up on tiptoes. Your spine and neck should be in a straight line, continuing through to your elbows. Once balanced, lean slowly forward until your head hovers over your hands. Drag yourself to the start position and continue.

Oppositional Arm and Leg Lifts

Lay face down on the floor with your arms above your head and your palms together (prayer style). Without moving your head or torso and keeping your shoulder from rotating, lift one arm off the floor a little, then lift the opposite leg, keeping the whole limb straight. Lower your arm, then your leg and copy the movements with your opposite arm and leg.

Buck Kick

Beginning in a classic press up position, make sure your feet are together and then kick off the floor, trying to push your heels back into your gluteus muscles. Snap back and land as gently as you can on your toes before repeating.

Handstand Press Up

Remember back at the top when I suggested working up to some of these exercises and possibly involving a friend? This is definitely one of those. While against a wall, invert your body so you're in handstand position then lower your body down the wall until your elbows are at right angles – I don't recommend letting your head take any weight! - then push your whole body up the wall again until your arms are straight. If you can, do another.

Martial Press Up

Another variation on the classic, this one begins in the press up starting position. From there, lift your buttocks up and quickly drop your torso to the floor until almost touching the carpet with your chin. Lift your head and shoulders, but keep your arms bent, while bringing your buttocks back down. Once complete, reverse the process until you're back to the start position.

Backward Flight

With your trusty water bottles as weights, stand straight with one foot in front of the other and your knees slightly bent. Your palms should be inwards and your core muscles tightened as you lean forwards, stretching your arms out sideways and using the muscles in your back to lift some of the weight. Repeat this a few times before switching leg positions and repeating again.

The Superman

It's up to you if you wear your undies on the outside and wear a cape but it'd really not necessary to do this exercise. Lay on your stomach with your hands outstretched over your head. While keeping your body as still as possible, lift both arms and legs up backwards as far as you can to make a flattened U shape. Hold the pose for half a minute and relax before going again.

Shoulder and Arm Exercises

Triceps Drop

You'll need a step or bench – although if you do it standing a low wall or table will do as well – to sit with your back towards. Bend your legs so your feet are flat on the floor. Reach back and grab the edge of whatever surface you're using and lift your body off the floor by straightening your arms. Drop down until your elbows make right angles but don't sit back down. Lift yourself up and down as many times as you can. Intensify this workout by lifting opposite arm and leg when you are at the lowest point of the rep.

Triangle Press Up

Yet *another* variation on a theme here, this version of the press up has you in the press up start position but with your hands underneath your face. Your index fingers and thumbs should be touching – to form a triangle – repositioning your hands like this give your triceps muscles an added workout.

Shadow Boxing

Stand with your feet under your shoulders and bend your knees a little. With your arms pulled tightly to your sides, lift one arm straight out in front of you and the other out backwards, making sure both arms form a straight line parallel to the floor. Keeping your elbows tucked in, return to the start position and alternate your arms.

IYTWO

What? You might think but bear with me on this one. Begin by laying face down on the floor with your arms above your head – the I position – then move to make the Y shape, followed by the T shape. The W shape is made by bending your elbows and lowering your shoulders, from the T position then put your hands together behind your back for the O.

Little Circles

You probably came across this as a form of punishment torture at school. Stand straight up and spread your arms out crucifix style. Rotate your hands from the shoulders, making small circles – about thirty centimeters in diameter is good – keep your arms straight and carry on for about half a minute. Reverse the direction of your circles for another half minute before switching back again.

Core Strengthening Exercises

L-Shape Seat

Similar in style to the triceps drop above, begin by sitting on the floor with your legs straight out, put your hands on the floor and lean forward slightly so your hands are slightly in front of the shoulders. Using your stomach muscles, lift your buttocks off the floor, tilting the pelvis up. Make sure you keep your arms locked so not to use them to do the lift, you want to use your abdominal muscles for this. Hold the pose for a few seconds then release and repeat.

Twisting Press Up

What? You ask, how many variations to the good old press up can there be? Millions! For this one you have to do a standard press up but when you get back up to the start position, reach up into the air while twisting your body at the same time. If you get this right, you should have one hand on the floor and be pointing up with the other hand, almost in the crucifix position. Drop back into the press up start position, do a normal press up then twist to the other side and extend the opposite arm.

Butterfly Kicks

Lay on your back with your hands slightly out from your sides, palms on the floor and legs straight out. Lift both legs off the floor and kick your feet up and down while keeping your legs straight. The action should all come from your hip joints, the power from your core muscles. Keep these small kicks up for a minute if you can.

Prone Plank Lifts

While in the plank pose, on forearms and toes, lift your buttocks up as far as you can while keeping your back as straight as possible. Do as many repetitions as you can.

Rotated Plank

Like it sounds, roll over on your side and raise your whole body on one elbow/forearm and the side of one foot. Make sure your hips are completely off the floor and hold the pose for half a minute to a minute – longer if you really feel good!

Cossack Twisting

Takes a good deal of balance this one. Sit on the floor with your legs together and raised off the floor. Your back should be at about a forty five degree angle and your buttocks will be the only thing touching the floor. You can use your arms for balance, then, without moving your legs, twist your arms from one side to the other. Go round as far as you can and take this one slowly as the slower you go the more effective it is.

The Cyclist

Laying on your back again – you'll get used to it – put your hands behind your head and pull your knees up toward your chest. Using alternate limbs, bring one elbow up towards the opposite knee and stretch out the other leg straight. So if you have your right elbow pointing at your left knee, your left leg should be straight (and still off the floor). Alternate the legs, bending your left knee and straightening your right.

Crunch

Another famous exercise here, but to get this one completely right, you need to concentrate on the position of your body. Lie on your back with your knees bent and your feet flat against the floor. Put your hands on the back of your head, dip your chin towards your chest and roll your head and shoulders up, using your abdominal muscles, until your lower back has left the floor. Hold this position for a couple of seconds before lowering yourself back down slowly.

Oblique Rotations

Sounds like it might be difficult this one but names can be deceptive. All you need to do for this simple, yet effective, exercise is lay flat on your back with knees bent and feet flat on the floor. Keeping those abdominal muscles tight, allow your knees to fall to the right until you can feel your oblique muscles stretch. Hold the position for five seconds and swap to the other side.

The Bridge

Lying (again) on your back with your knees bent and your feet flat on the floor, leave your arms at your sides and lift your back and buttocks off the floor. Your spine should not be bent and the only contact points with the floor should be your feet, shoulders arms and head. Once up, lift one leg, keeping your abdominal muscles tight, lower it slowly back down and repeat, changing legs after about ten reps.

Individual Leg Abdominal Presses

Laid on your back (!) with feet flat on the ground and knees bent, bring your right leg up at the hip to create a right angle. Using the palm of your right hand, press down on your right knee to create pressure for your abdominal muscles. After five seconds holding this, relax and swap to the other leg. For added fun, you can do a double leg abdominal press, bringing up both knees and pressing your hands down at the same time.

Runner's Sit Ups

Lie on your back with your legs straight out and your arms beside you on the floor, elbows bent at right angles so your forearms stick straight up. Then sit up while lifting your right knee towards your left elbow, lay back down and swap sides, alternating for ten to twenty repetitions.

Some DON'Ts of Squatting

Just a few little health and safety tips to avoid any injury to your leg muscles.

- Don't let your back assume a crouch. Keep your chest tight and front facing, eyes straight and shoulder blades back.

- Don't use the balls of your feet to get back to the original position. Instead take help of the curling tendency of your feet to achieve the same. Unnecessary pressure on the tendons and joints may prove harmful for you.
- Don't let your hips move faster than your shoulder blades. Bring a sort of synchrony between the two parts of your body.
- Don't allow your knees to protrude forward farther than is necessary. This happens when your hips are not under your full control. Once you gain a balance between the movement of your knees and the movement of your hips, you are good to go.
- Don't make the mistake of looking down, as it will simply lead to curving of your spine. Some people also make the mistake of half-squatting or pseudo-squatting by not trying hard enough to make their thighs parallel to the ground.

Weekends have always been synonymous with fun and frolic, so it's advisable to not work out during this period of time. Despite how leisurely you feel, do not give in to the temptation of working out. Some people get obsessed with exercising due to the 'happy hormones' it releases. This must be avoided, not every day should be dedicated to developing your body. Rest over the weekends as your body needs some respite from the heavy working out it has been subjected to over the week.

Chapter 5

Weight Loss and Nutrition Myths – Busted

How many times have you seen these claims? "Lose 10 lbs. in just 10 days!" Eat what you want, as much as you want and still drop those pounds!" or "try this latest diet/exercise/supplement and lose inches of your waist/thighs/tummy fast!" More than once, I'll wager a very large bet!

The thing is, there are so many diets and so many different tools being shoved down our throats these days it is very difficult to determine what works and what doesn't – or even what to believe! So, to help you out, I am going to go over a few myths about diet, weight loss, exercise and nutrition. My aim is to help you to make more healthy choices and changes in your life, so that when you are bombarded with advertisements you can work out which ones are real and which ones should just be treated with the disdain they deserve!

Diet Myths

Myth – Fad diets really work! I'll lose weight and keep it off easily!

This really isn't going to happen. Fad diets are just that – fads and, although you may see a quick weight loss initially, it won't last. These types of diet tend to restrict what you eat, in both amount and food types and is inordinately hard to stick to. Because they are so restrictive, most people fail to stick to them almost immediately. There is a good reason for this – many of the fad diets out there are sorely lacking in the balance of nutrients, proteins, carbohydrates, vitamins, minerals, and everything else you need to keep yourself healthy. Not only that, fast weight losses of 3 or more pounds per week can lead to gallstones and if you are eating less than 800 calories per day for a long period of time, you are increasing your risk of heart problems.

The safest and best way to lose weight is to eat less calories than you are burning off through physical activity but to make sure that those calories contain all you need to be fit and healthy. Aim for ½ to 1 pound per week in weight loss and eat smaller portions more often, instead of just three meals a day. Exercise daily and you will see the pounds and inches start to drop off and you will also be reducing your risk of heart problems, diabetes, strokes and high blood pressure.

Myth – Grains are fattening so I should avoid eating pasta, bread and rice if I want to lose weight

Grain products are those that are made from rice, wheat, oats, cornmeal, barley or any other cereal grain. They are divided into two groups – refined and whole grains. The whole grains contain the whole kernel, examples being: whole wheat bread and brown rice. Whereas refined grain has been milled, and the wheatgerm and bran have been removed from them. The reason for the milling is to refine the texture and give the product a much longer shelf life. Unfortunately, it also removes the iron, most of the B vitamins and the dietary fiber that are present in the whole grains.

There is nothing wrong with eating whole grains and indeed, you may even lower your chances of developing a chronic disease if you eat it on a daily basis. It is very easy to make the necessary changes to your diet – instead of white bread, pick up whole grain or, instead of white rice, go for brown, the same with pasta.

One of the best ways to lose weight is follow an eating plan that is healthy and contains fruit, vegetables, whole grains, dairy and protein. Cut down on refined sugar, salt, saturated fats, cholesterol, and increase the amount of protein you eat. And that leads us nicely to the next myth.

Myth – Some people can eat as much as they like and never put on any weight

We all know that to lose weight we have to burn off more calories than we actually eat (see above) but some people do appear to be able to eat anything they want and in any quantity they want without putting on any weight at all. Those people, if you take a look at their lifestyle, are burning off huge amounts of energy throughout the day and, as such, can get away with it. One of the best ways to ensure that you are eating a healthy diet is to eat the rainbow. When you have a meal, make sure that at least half of your plate is filled with fruits and vegetables and always go for the vibrant ones as these contain more minerals, vitamins and fiber, not to mention antioxidants and are far better for you:

- **Red** – Bell peppers, cranberries, cherries, onions, strawberries, red beets, watermelon, tomatoes
- **Green** – Avocado, cabbage, broccoli, dark lettuce, cucumber, honeydew melon, grapes, kale, spinach, kiwi, zucchini

- **Orange and Yellow -** Banana, apricot, carrots, oranges, mangoes, peaches, squash, sweet potatoes
- **Blue and Purple** – blueberries, blackberries, grapes, purple cabbage, plums, purple carrots, purple potatoes

Be aware that, although you can still consume your favorite foods while following a healthy eating plan, you must make sure you count the calories and include them as part of your daily limit – don't fall into the trap of substituting healthy foods with junk food too much though – it won't work! Reduce your portion sizes down and find ways of keeping the calorie count of your favorite foods down. For example, instead of frying something, grill or bake it instead. Ditch the cream, replace it with low fat milk – or yoghurt if cooking – instead, and always make sure that half of your meal plate consists of fruit and vegetables.

Myth – Low fat or no fat foods don't contain any calories

Everything contains calories, even a plain lettuce leaf, it's just that foods that are lower in fat may contain less than the full fat version. Do be aware that processed foods that claim to be low or no fat still contain just as many calories, if not more. They will also contain added ingredients such as salt, flour, sugar or starch to give them a better flavor and texture after the fat is taken out – and all of these added extras contain calories.

Some people get confused between a serving and a portion. A serving is a recommended amount. If you look on the side of the box or can, you will find a food nutrition label, which tells you the number of calories and servings per box, or can. The serving size will vary with each product. A portion, on the other hand, is how much you decide to eat at any one time and that doesn't always match with the serving size.

The food nutrition label is a handy tool provided it is used properly. You can use it to track how many servings you have, your calorie intake and to determine which foods are lower in fat, sugar and salt and higher in the good stuff like dietary fiber and vitamins.

How to Read a Nutrition Label

At the top of the label, you will always see the serving size and how many servings are in the container of food product.

Below that, the number of calories per serving size will be listed, followed by the ingredients, listed in order of the largest percentage down to the smallest. Fats, cholesterol and sodium should be limited in your diet and protein, carbohydrate and minerals and vitamins should be increased. So make sure you know how to read the label correctly to determine what you are eating.

NOTE – please be aware that the percentages are per serving size, not the entire contents of the packet, unless the packet is one single serving.

Myth – Fast foods are unhealthy and should be avoided at all costs on a diet

Yes, many fast foods are very unhealthy and will result in weight gain. However, more and more fast food places are now offering healthier options for you to choose from. Make sure you choose those that are low in salt, sugar and calories and are rich in nutrients, as well as being small portion sizes. The menu will often tell you the nutritional facts about food or you can sometimes find it on the website for the restaurant. Please keep in mind that the nutritional facts will not include any information about sauces or extras. The following tips may help you:

- Try to avoid going for the combo meals. Although they may represent good value for money, they are higher in calories
- For dessert, go for fresh fruit or yoghurt – nonfat preferably
- Limit how much topping you have if it is high in calories and fat – cheese and bacon are two good

examples, as are full fat mayonnaise, tartar sauce and salad dressings (unless made with lemon and olive oil)

- Choose steamed foods or baked foods instead of fried
- Instead of the calorie and sugar laden sodas, choose water or fat free milk

Myth – Skipping meals will make me lose weight

Unfortunately, the reverse is true. Skipping a meal tends to make you feel hungrier which leads to you snacking on bad foods or eating more than you should at your next meal. Breakfast is the worst meal of the day to skip. Breakfast is the meal that kick starts your metabolism and helps you to burn off fat faster. The following tips will help you to ensure you are not skipping meals and are eating a good healthy variety:

- Make a quick breakfast of oatmeal, made with low fat milk and topped off with fresh berries. You could also eat a slice of whole grain toast with a sugar free fruit spread
- Pack up your lunch the night before and make sure it is a healthy one. Making it the night before will help you to avoid the temptation of spinning out of the door in the morning without it.

- Pack up a healthy low-fat yogurt, vegetables with hummus or whole wheat crackers with peanut butter as healthy snacks.

Myth – Good healthy food is too expensive

Changing your diet for the better does not necessarily mean having to spend more money. You also don't need to fall into the trap of buying only fresh foods – they don't always contain more nutrients or goodness than the frozen or canned variety. Spinach for example contains as much goodness frozen as it does fresh – and it lasts longer as well as being cheaper. There are plenty of canned or frozen options that are low in salt and sugar – just remember to read the labels. Do rinse anything that has been canned to remove the excess salt from it. You can also keep canned seafood, such as mackerel, tuna and salmon, on the shelf, ready for when you want it, instead of spending a fortune on fresh. Lastly, canned or frozen beans, peas, and lentils are also healthy and easy to keep, as well as being cheaper.

When you are buying canned foods, check for those that are in water or their own juice. Also, check for foods that are high in potassium, calcium, fiber, vitamin D and protein, as well as being low in added sugars or salt. Tuna should come in brine rather than vegetable oil.

Physical Activity Myths

Too many of us spend too much time sitting down, leading to a rise in obesity and heart diseases. Make time to move during the day and get some regular activity, preferably aerobic that makes your heart beat faster, your breath faster and sweat to run.

Myth – Weight lifting won't help me lose weight, it will just bulk out my muscles

Bodyweight exercises like crunches and pushups on a regular basis will certainly help your muscles to build up but this is a good thing. Stronger muscles burn off more calories, resulting in weight loss. To make your muscles stronger using bodyweight exercises, do pushups or sit-ups 2 or 3 times a week and get out do some yard work as well, tasks like digging that make you work hard. This level of activity will not bulk you out – the only way to do that is through intense training.

Adults should be exercising at least twice a week to strengthen up their muscles as well as between 150 and 300 minutes of aerobic activity every week – vigorous or intense, like brisk walking or cycling, enough to make you sweat.

Myth – Physical activity doesn't count if it is only done for a short period of time

Any physical activity counts, not just long periods of time and it really doesn't take many short periods of activity to build up your 150 to 300 minutes a week. The experts say that you should spend at least 10 minutes at a time on aerobic activity but that could just be a brisk walk to the shop and back, or getting off the train a stop earlier.

Try to do 10 minutes of aerobic activity three times a day on at least 5 days of the week to meet the 150-minute goal. It doesn't matter what it is, as long as it is brisk, makes your heart beat rise, you're breathing faster and it makes you sweat.

Food Myths

Myth – Meat is bad for you and eating it makes it harder to lose weight

Eating lean meat in measured amounts is a good part of a healthy diet because it gives you the protein without too much of the fat. Protein is essential for building muscles and repairing damage to your body. While chicken, pork, fish, and red meats do contain cholesterol and saturated fats, they also contain vital nutrients like protein, iron and zinc.

Aim for cuts that are lean and lower in fat and then cut off any fat that is on the meat. Lower fat meats include chicken breast, beef round steak, pork loin, extra lean ground beef and flank steak. Do watch how much you eat as well – stick to a portion size of 3 ounces or less.

Myth – Dairy products are not healthy and they are fattening

Not all dairy is bad for you; low fat and no fat yoghurts, milk and cheese are as healthy as whole milk and they are much lower in calories and fat. Dairy contains protein, which again is needed for building up those muscles and helping your organs to work, as they should, and it also contains calcium, which helps to strengthen up bones. Some yoghurts and most milk has vitamin D added in which is essential to help your body use the calcium efficiently.

Aim to have 3 cups per day of low fat or no fat milk or milk products, including soy drinks, which have been fortified with added vitamins. If you are lactose intolerant, i.e. you can't digest the lactose in dairy, opt for low, no lactose products, or other products that contain both calcium and vitamin D, such as:

- **Calcium** – soy based products, tofu that has been made with calcium sulfate, canned salmon and dark leafy greens, such as spinach, kale and collards
- **Vitamin D** – Soy based drinks and fortified cereals

Myth – Giving up meat and going vegetarian will help me to lose weight faster and be healthier

Research and studies have shown that vegetarians do tend to eat less fat and less calories than those who eat meat and/or fish. Some of those studies have also found that vegetarianism may be linked to lower levels of obesity, a lower risk of heart disease and lower blood pressure. Vegetarians also tend to have lower BM (body mass index) scores than non-vegetarians. However, being vegetarian does not automatically mean you are eating any more healthily or any more likely to lose weight faster.

Vegetarians can very easily make food choices that cause them to pile on the weight instead of losing it by eating foods that are high in calories and fat and lower in nutrients. There are different types of vegetarian diets – vegans do not eat any animal product while a lacto-ovo vegetarian will eat eggs and milk with a diet of plant food. Some vegetarians allow themselves to eat small amounts of seafood, meat and poultry as well but live mainly on a vegetable and plant food diet.

If you opt for a vegetarian lifestyle, you must ensure that you are taking in enough of the nutrients that non-vegetarians would get from animal foods, like meat, cheese and eggs. Nutrients that may be in low supply in a vegetarian diet are shown below along with ideas for foods that may help you to meet the daily requirement:

- **Calcium** – dairy, soy with added calcium, collards, kale, broccoli, tofu made with calcium sulfate
- **Iron** – Spinach cashew nuts chickpeas, lentils, bread, cereal with iron added
- **Protein** - dairy, eggs, peas, beans, nuts, tempeh, tofu, soy burgers
- **Vitamin B12** - eggs, dairy, soy beverages or cereals that have been fortified, miso, tempeh – both of these are made from soybeans
- **Vitamin D** - milk, soy drinks, cereals and any other foods that have added vitamin D
- **Zinc** - whole grain*, tofu, nuts, leafy greens like lettuce, spinach and cabbage

* Make sure you check the nutritional facts label to see that the words “whole grain” or “whole” have been added in front of the grain ingredient name

Chapter 6

The Importance of Recovery Time Between Sessions

Most athletes are fully aware of the need for rest after exercising and they also know that sufficient rest is vital if they are to increase their performance. However, despite this, many still train too hard and too much and feel pangs of guilt when they take a day out and rest. The body needs a period of rest to help it to heal and repair, as well as strengthening up between workout sessions. A continuous train of working out without enough rest can do serious and, in some cases, irreparable damage to the body. There are a number of reasons why rest days are vital to performance, some psychological and some physiological but the main ones are to let your mind recover and allow your muscles time to repair, heal and strengthen up.

What Happens to my Body During Recovery?

The importance of adding recovery time into your workout program cannot be stressed enough. This time is when your body starts to adapt to the stress it has endured during the exercise and this is when the real effects of your hard training take effect. Recovery also allows your energy stores to be refilled and damaged tissues get the chance to repair themselves. Any physical work causes a number of changes in your body, including the breakdown of muscle tissue and energy stores (muscle glycogen) being depleted from your muscles, not to mention loss of fluid.

Adding in sufficient recovery time allows these stores to be refilled and gives body tissues the chance to repair themselves. If you do not allow sufficient time, your body will continue breaking down from the intensive work it has been put through and that s when symptoms of over-training begin to manifest themselves. Those symptoms include becoming stale, a general feeling of malaise, depression, an increase in the risk of injury, a decrease in performance and many more besides.

Short and Long Term Recovery

There are two recovery categories – short and long term. The short-term recovery is immediate – when you rest after a hard training session – and the long term is the recovery sessions that need to be built in over a course of time. Both types are important for optimal performance and peak fitness.

Short-term recovery is often called active recovery and it happens in the hours that follow on from an exercise session. Active recovery refers to the engagement of low impact exercise after a hard workout and in the days that follow. Both types are important for performance. One of the biggest reasons for this recovery is to replenish your energy stores and lost fluids as well as optimizing the process of protein synthesis – this is when the protein content in the muscle cells is increased, to help stop the muscles from breaking down while helping to increase the size of your muscles - this is done by consuming the right kind of foods during the recovery session. This is also the time when your muscles, ligaments and tendons repair themselves and the chemicals that have built up through the activity of cells during the exercise are removed from your body. One part of the recovery process that is often overlooked s the need for enough quality sleep. It isn't enough to sleep for 8 hours every night if that sleep is light and interrupted. It is far better to sleep for 6 hours if that sleep is relaxed and uninterrupted and you wake feeling refreshed. Long-term recovery is built into your training schedule and will include complete days or weeks set aside for rest from exercising and training.

The Principle of Adaptation

This principle declares that, as we put our bodies through the stress of exercise and physical work, our bodies will begin to adapt and to become far more efficient. It is the same as learning anything new – to start with, it may be hard but, as you practice and as time goes by, it becomes second nature to you. Once you and your body have adapted to a specific stress, you need more of that stress to make any more progress.

However, the human body does have limits on how much stress it can take before it begins breaking down and increasing your risk of injury. Doing too much exercise in too short a time will result in injury or damage to your muscles but, conversely, doing too little too slowly will not show any improvement at all. This is why you need a proper training program that increases in intensity and time, as well as incorporating proper recovery times.

Sleep Deprivation is Bad for You

If you have a night or two of bad sleep it won't have too much of an impact on your performance but if you consistently sleep badly or have too many long nights and too little sleep, you will begin to notice changes in your hormone levels. In particular, the hormones that are related to stress, mood, and muscle recovery are the worst affected. Nobody can completely understand the complexities of sufficient quality sleep, there is some research that shows sleep deprivation will increase cortisol levels (stress hormone), decreases how active the human growth hormone is (this is very active while the tissues are repairing) and also decreases the glycogen synthesis.

Learn to Balance your Exercise with Recovery and Rest

It is learning how to efficiently alternate exercise with rest and recovery that will take your performance to a higher level and maximize your results. It is important to realize that the more intense your training, the bigger the need there is for planned recovery times. You should get into the habit of monitoring your exercise sessions by using a training journal and monitoring how your body feels and your motivation levels. This is important for determining your recovery needs and making necessary changes to your training plan to ensure you get sufficient rest and recovery periods.

10 Ways to Recover From Exercise Quickly

There are lots of ways to recover but the following ten are recommended by training experts:

1. **Replace Lost Fluids**

When you exercise, you will lose a lot of fluid from your body. In an ideal world, you would replace it as you exercise but, if you cannot, then filling up on fluid after exercise is just as good. Drink water not fruit juices, tea, coffee or any other beverage. Water is vital for supporting every single metabolic function and transfer of nutrients in your body and having sufficient quantities of water will help to improve all of your bodily functions. Proper replacement of fluids is particularly important for endurance athletes who tend to lose large quantities of water through sweating for hours.

2. **Eat Properly**

Through exercise, your energy stores will be depleted and must be replenished. Your body needs to be refueled if you want it to recover fully, your tissues to repair properly and to get stronger, ready for the next round. This is especially important if you are doing endurance exercises every day or are trying to build up your muscles. You should try to eat within one hour of finishing your session and ensure that you eat high quality complex carbohydrates and proteins.

3. **Stretch Properly**

I told you at the start you needed to warm up before a workout to avoid damaging your muscles, well it is equally as important to cool down afterward as well. As soon as your exercise session is over, it is important to stretch your muscles gently. This will reduce the risk of cramping and injury and will also help your muscles to recover fully.

4. **Rest**

When you are ill or have an injury, you rest because it makes you feel better. The same applies to your body after exercise. Rest is essential to allow your body the time to recover itself and heal.

5. **Active Recovery**

Easy movement after exercise helps to improve circulation and that helps to move nutrients around the body quickly and remove waste products from the body in a more efficient way. This is also said to help your muscles repair and heal much quicker. Go for a gentle walk after exercising or a gentle lazy swim.

6. **Go for a Massage**

Massage helps to improve circulation and it feels good as well, helping you to relax your mind and body fully. You can try self-massage using foam rollers or book in for a session of sports massage at your local gym.

7. **Have an Ice Bath**

Many athletes swear by using ice to help them recover quicker. They use ice baths, ice massage or contrast showers, which is alternating hot and cold water. This also helps to reduce soreness in the muscles and prevent injury. The theory behind using ice and heat is that the action of dilating and constricting the blood vessels repeatedly helps to remove waste products from the tissues. To use the contrast therapy, take a shower after your exercise session and alternate with 2 minutes of hot water followed by 30 seconds of cold and then one minute of moderate temperature water. Repeat this four times for maximum benefit.

8. **Get Sufficient Sleep**

When you sleep, your body and brain continue to work, producing amazing results. Good sleep is a requirement for anyone who does exercise on a regular basis. While you sleep, GH (growth hormone) is released, helping your tissues to repair and grow, aiding quicker recovery and a reduced risk of injury

9. **Don't Over train**

The simplest way to recover from your session quicker is not to over train. Draw up a smart plan and avoid excessive heavy training in each session; ensure adequate rest time is included in your plan to ensure you gain in both fitness and recovery.

10. Utilize Meditation, Imagery and Visualization

Adding mental practices to your physical routine will benefit you immensely. Mental practices can result in a clearer mind, a clear and calm attitude and less anxiety.

Meditation

If you're new to the whole idea of meditation, here are a few pointers to steer you in the right direction to help both your body and mind recover while getting the most from your bodyweight training.

Find somewhere you are at peace to begin with. There should be as little to distract you as possible to begin with, you can learn to tune things out at a later stage. The space you choose doesn't have to be massive or plushly decorated, as long as there is somewhere you can sit quietly and peacefully to focus on your meditation. Your bedroom, a closet, even your office at work will all be fine as long as it's somewhere you can get away from distractions and interruptions for as long as you plan to meditate.

If you are a novice at meditating, it's even more important to eliminate the amount of distractions there might be. So unplug the TV, switch your cellphone to silent – or, dare I say it, switch it off – take the batteries out of the radio and make sure all kitchen appliances or chainsaws are stored safely away. The space you use does not have to be completely silent, but make sure, if you want music in there, it is music which enhances your experience rather than distracting you from what you are here for. If music is not your thing, you might want to try one of those indoor water features you can buy, the sound of running water can be immensely soothing – just make sure you have used the bathroom first.

Along with this knowledge you need not be in complete silence, you should also know that someone's dog barking or someone else cutting their grass a few houses up should not distract you enough to ruin your meditation. If you are aware of, but not distracted by, these occasional noises, it will eventually increase the effectiveness of your meditation.

This is also true of those who choose to meditate in the open air, as many people choose to do. Obviously you can't stop other people from using a public space or driving past your garden, so unless you live on a massive ranch in the middle of nowhere, there are likely to be some sounds to get used to. If you do want to meditate outside, you should still try to find somewhere you find peaceful, on some nicely scented grass or under a tree for some shade.

As meditation is a personal thing, it really does not matter where you choose to practice, as long as it is a peaceful space to *you* it will work. If you find the beach a soothing environment, go there, in a forest? Find one you can get to easily and grab a seat.

In order to get the most from your meditation, especially at the beginning, you should choose to wear clothes which do not chafe or pull. The basic concept of meditation is to help calm your mind and forget the world around you, which can be hard to do if your jeans are so tight they are cutting into your legs. Where possible wear light fitting, loose clothing. Make sure you will be warm enough, if meditating outside, or the distraction of shivering in the cold will ruin your meditation. Take your shoes off so there can be no possibility of feeling the hardness of their construction which might put you off and break your concentration. If you are planning to meditate at work and cannot wear, or change into, loose clothes – many offices look down on stripping in the middle of the day to meditate – at least you can take a few steps to make the clothes you have on more comfortable. Take off any jacket or blazer you are wearing, loosen or remove that tie and undo your belt too.

You need now to decide how long to meditate for. Masters of the technique will tell you to meditate for at least twenty minutes a couple of times a day but someone new to this can begin with five minutes a day and build your time up – a little like adding more time to your workout routines.

You should also aim to meditate at the same time every day. If you meditate for ten minutes just before breakfast or during your lunch break from work, make sure you meditate at the same time to work it into your daily routine.

So now you have a time of day and length of meditation session figured out, make sure you actually do it. If you give up on this because you think it's a waste of time or not for you, chances are you will also stop your bodyweight training. Meditation is a learned process and like all learned things will take time to master, just keep at it and you can achieve success.

Even though you want to keep an eye on the time you are spending while in meditation, resist the temptation to keep looking at your watch as this counts as another distraction. In fact I recommend taking your watch off and setting an alarm – possibly on your phone – or getting someone to gently rouse you.

So you are ready to begin your meditation? Not quite, there are a few more little tips for you to get the absolute most from your meditation. To start with do a few stretches. Spending a few minutes getting your body ready to sit still for a while is a very good idea as this will get rid of the distraction caused by any tense muscles you might have.

To begin with, stretch and flex your neck and shoulders – this is particularly good for office workers hunched over a computer – then move on to your lower back. It is also a good idea to stretch your leg muscles especially if you are going to meditate in the lotus position. You do not have to spend hours on these stretches, just be aware they do facilitate the whole process and, especially for beginners, can help in meditation.

Seat yourself comfortably. Comfort is essential and you have to bear in mind you do not have to immediately leap into the lotus position and stay there regardless of how much it might hurt. Flexibility and strength will come through your bodyweight training. If at the start you are not quite flexible enough to remain in this position for long enough to achieve your meditation goals, sit cross-legged, in the half-lotus position - place only one foot on top of the opposite leg and leave the other in cross legged position – or even on a chair. Meditation is a personal journey, so take the information available and adapt it to your own personal circumstances. Whatever the seating position you choose to adopt, bear in mind you need some kind of cushion or pad which allows your pelvis to tilt forwards so your spine can be aligned and you sit upright. On a chair, put something (length of wood or plastic, old books) under the back legs which is three or four inches thick. Sitting on the edge of a pad or cushion you need to get your spine aligned above the pair of bony protrusions in your backside this will allow your spine to take the weight of your upper body, as it is supposed to.

It will take some practice to get each of the vertebrae in your back to line up perfectly so your entire upper body and head is supported. The aim here is to use as little muscular power as possible to support you, in effect switching off completely.

Traditionally, your hands should rest on your lap or thighs, with your palms facing upwards and your right hand sitting on your left. Again this is all down to personal choice and you can let your hands rest anywhere, even dangling at your sides, as long as it is a relaxed position.

Next it is a good idea to close your eyes, while you can meditate with your eyes open, there are visual distractions which are more likely to put off a beginner. Eventually, after you are comfortable with the process of meditation, you can attempt meditation with your eyes open. This can be helpful for a number of reasons: if you find yourself falling asleep, if you discover you are concentrating too much on the process of meditation – which can be distracting in itself – or if, like a small percentage of people, you experience nightmarish images.

Concentrate on your breathing to begin with, this is one of the most fundamental meditation techniques to master and is probably the best place to begin your meditation practice. Once you feel you are relaxed and seated correctly, imagine a spot just above your belly button and bring your mind to bear on that spot. Register the rise and all of that spot as you take a breath and release it. Breathe as you normally would and do not make any changes in the way you breathe.

Attempt to concentrate on your breathing and only that. Try not to think about the process of breathing – do not count or measure your breaths – simply try and be *aware* of your breathing, to know you *are* breathing. It can be helpful to visualize something as you try this. Imagine there is a coin above your belly button which goes up and down with the ebb and flow of your breath. Possibly try thinking of a ball floating in the sea which rises and falls in time with your breathing.

You might find your concentration wandering, you are a beginner after all, and this all takes practice. If your attention does wander, try and get refocused back on the task in hand – concentrate on that spot above your belly button and try again.

Empty your mind. Effective meditation calls for only concentrating on one thing. As a beginner, you might find it helpful to focus on one single thing, such as a simple mantra or object. Eventually you will learn to completely clear your mind.

Mantras

To use a mantra – which is a single sound, word or phrase – you just repeat your chosen mantra again and again until your conscious mind calms and you enter a meditative state. As long as you choose a mantra which you can remember easily, you can use anything. I would suggest a single word such as 'one', 'tranquil', 'calm', 'peace' or 'quiet' although single syllable words are often easier. You could also choose the often heard 'Om', this stands for a consciousness which is omnipresent.

Mantras are supposed to be tools for your mind and are also similar to musical instruments which set up vibrations in your consciousness. In turn, these vibrations help you cut off your surface mind and go into a much deeper level of consciousness.

While repeating your chosen mantra over in your head, let the word, phrase or sound, reverberate through your conscious mind. If you lose focus or are distracted from this, do not worry, just try and concentrate again, continuing to repeat your mantra. Eventually you will go into a deeper level of your mind and probably not need to carry on repeating your chosen mantra.

If you choose to use a visual object on which to concentrate, while dropping into a deeper level of your conscious mind, use something simple. Again this is down to personal choice and can be anything you want, many people find the flickering flame of a candle is the best form of visual aid, however other things which can be used are stones or crystals and small statues of spiritual significance.

Begin with your chosen item level with your eyes, you do not want to have to stretch your neck to look at it. Then stare at that object, looking at nothing else and allowing nothing else to enter your vision. When mastered this technique should allow your vision to fade down so your whole mind is focused on the given object. When you have become so focused on the object nothing else enters your mind you should become totally calm and at peace.

Another type of meditation is known as visualization and involves building a peaceful place in your mind. Once you have entered this fictitious place you begin looking around and exploring it until you reach a completely serene state.

Again, the place you build needs to be absolutely personal to you. You could choose a sun drenched beach, a cool, still forest, beside a stream or floating on clouds. While you can draw from reality, I suggest injecting a sense of the fantastic or surreal. This allows you to make the transition from the surface of your conscious mind to the deeper areas.

Now you are in your special place you can begin to look about. Do not try to build or add to your environment, everything should already be there, just let the things which make the place up, no matter how far out or fantastic, appear in your mind. Let the sights and smells of your paradise come to you, if you are outside in your paradise, let the sun warm you or the gentle wind cool you. Listen to the sounds which run through the place, birds chirping, waves washing against the shore or the musical trickle of water in a stream or river.

Revel and enjoy in your space for as long as you want and let it grow while you do so without thinking about it. Eventually when you want to come back to the real world slowly let your eyes open, secure in the knowledge you can always go back to that serene paradise again. It will always exist inside your mind in whatever form you choose to keep it. It is your 'safe' place and no one can change or take it from you except you. If you want to alter it, you can, there are no rules here, whatever makes you feel at peace the most.

Body Scanning

This is a process where you concentrate on different areas of your body individually and making sure you relax them. This form of meditation lets you relax your body – which is the point of this section of the book – at the same time as you relax your mind.

Begin by closing your eyes and selecting a starting point, usually at the bottom of your body, the feet and toes. Focus on the feelings and sensations you can feel coming from your feet and try to relax your toes as much as possible to relieve any tension in the muscles there. Turn your attention to your feet next and relax those next. Work up through your body, section by section: lower legs and knees, thighs, bottom, hip joints, abdominal muscles, chest, back, shoulders and biceps, elbows and forearms, wrists and fingers. Finish up with your neck and face, moving up to your scalp – Yes it does move, have muscles in and can be tensed!

Taking your time, concentrate on your whole body, reveling in the complete sense of relaxation and calm you have reached. Go back to the top and concentrate on your breathing for a while until you are ready to end your meditation.

Heart Chakra Meditation

Your body is said to have seven chakras throughout your body and the heart chakra can be found in the middle of your chest. Linked with feelings of love, peace and compassion, this type of meditation concerns engaging these feelings and transmitting them out into the world.

Begin this by shutting your eyes then rub your hands together which brings warmth and energy to the surface. Putting your right hand in the middle of your chest, over the heart chakra, lay your left hand on top of your right. Breathe deeply in and then out slowly, saying 'yam' with your breath as you do. 'Yam' holds an association with your heart chakra and the vibrations which come from it. While you do all this, imagine green glowing energy coming from your chest being absorbed by your hands.

This green energy represents all the positive feelings you are experiencing at the time. When you feel the time is right, lift your hands off your chest and let the energy dissipate from your hands and out into the world.

Try and feel the energy which surrounds your body, especially in your limbs, do not panic if you cannot feel it, just imagine the energy you use to move your body, it is field of energy which surrounds and imbues you.

The Power of Positive Thinking

My grandfather was a really positive inspiration on my life, never knowing my own dad I automatically looked at him as a role model. Now I'm not going to say he was a perfect specimen of manhood, he had his moments, when life tried him and got him down, who doesn't? What I am willing to say is that as a teenager he lost his left leg above the knee and even though he had very little formal education, he managed to have a career, family and home which was owned outright way before the time he died.

I on the other hand was a maudlin, overweight child with access to a full education system and completely functional working body. And complaints. Still, he never seemed to lose patience with me, never lost his temper – with me at least – and always gave me the following advice, no matter how he worded it.

"Everything depends on your attitude. If that's what you believe, then that's how things will be." and "Moaning about it won't make any difference, you have to do something to change it."

At which point – being a miserable teen – I'd get annoyed, wondering exactly what kind of rubbish he was trying to peddle. He expected me to think about life in a different way and things will all get better. Now I'm older – not telling you how old so don't ask – I realize that's pretty much how it works.

Industrialist Henry – Model T – Ford once said,

"No matter whether you think you can do something ir you think you can't, you're right."

Really, it *is* as simple as that – your thoughts decide your actions – but it is much harder to believe in a real world setting. Yet whether you believe it or not, the way in which you think about yourself and your life can seriously increase your amount of happiness and reduce your stress. How you think about things can even have a positive, or negative, effect on gaining your goals. So having an optimistic outlook on life *will* help cement your success, while negativity is the absolute bane to your success.

Consider the successful entrepreneurs in the world – Sir Richard Branson, Bill Gates, Steve Jobs to name a few you have probably heard of – many people think the secret to the massive successes of these people are their positive outlooks on life and the way they strive constantly to achieve their goals.

Gandhi explained things in a lifelong existence,

"Make sure your thoughts remain positive as your thoughts become your words. Make sure your words remain positive as your words become your behavior.

Make sure your behavior remains positive as your behavior becomes your habits. Make sure your habits remain positive as your habits become your values. Make sure your values remain positive as your values become your destiny."

The point is if you cannot or will not believe the power of positive thinking – or at least the possibility of it – you are actually making the decision to be negative. I expect you are even now thinking of a number of reasons why these words are wrong and you can name plenty of times in your life when thinking positively did not make a bit of difference.

Any idea why? (And you possibly will not like this)

It is simply because you enjoy being negative and you enjoy being negative because it takes away any responsibility for the actions and choices you make. A negative mind will invent any number of scenarios to explain why things are going wrong – it is a kind of self-preservation. Your mind will tell you you were passed over for that job because there is a storm cloud hovering over your whole life. You are unlucky or cannot get a break from your bad luck, horrible things always seem to happen to you.

This type of detrimental thought process will always enable you to blame someone or something else for the failures you have experienced. At the same time it is blinding you from actually seeing the really good things there are in your life.

So how do you get back control and use the power of positive thought. It is so ridiculously easy to begin, you will probably start off by thinking it cannot possibly work. (See what I did there?)

Grab a piece of paper and write down a few little goals you want to achieve through bodyweight training. Not massive things like having a perfectly sculpted athletic body, that comes later – although you can do it – but simple, short term things like sticking to your workout routine. Make sure you write whatever it is an a positive way,

"I will work out five days in seven for at least an hour."

You can add as much to this as you want but bear in mind, you need to read it, time and time again until your brain accepts it. This is the only technique I have found which works almost all of the time for anyone.

Keep this piece of paper with you at all times – in your wallet, purse or pocket – and read it, aloud if you can, to yourself at least three times a day. Just after you wake, at lunch and before you go to sleep work best. Do not feel you need to limit yourself to three times a day, if you can read it every hour then do that, you will eventually find yourself simply thinking this way without the need for the paper.

Add to the list of things you want to achieve – with regards to bodyweight training and other things in your life – after all, what have you got to lose? If you think negatively and things do not go your way it is a 'self-fulfilling prophesy'. If you think positively and achieve nothing, you have wasted nothing except for your negative thoughts (and who wants those anyway?) but if you think positively and achieve your goals – which I know you will – think of how good it will make you feel and how that feeling of euphoria will push you into believing you can do more if only you think you *can*.

Make sure you do set those goals, though, if you have no goals to work towards, you cannot achieve anything. Do not over achieve though, pick a simple goal and start working towards it.

Remember to imagine yourself achieving the goal, your body cannot get to a place your mind cannot imagine. Once you have had one success, keep repeating how it felt when you did achieve it, how good it was to get to where you wanted to be and all with the help of positive thought.

Another point to make here is that you have to be completely self-reliant on controlling your mind. No one else can influence the way you think – even though they might try – you are the master of your own mind and if you tell it to behave a certain way, it will do so. In combination with bodyweight training and the meditation techniques above, you are well on your way to being the master of your own destiny.

Do not blame external forces for your failings in life, no longer accept there is nothing you can do to change things. If the smallest aspect of your life is not right for you, it is down to you to change it, no one else can or even should. You cannot allow yourself any more negativity, no more thinking, 'I can't do this,' or 'I've got no idea how,' You are completely capable of learning how to do something you are unfamiliar with, we all are, the only barrier to not learning it is your own mind and negative thoughts.

One harsh lesson you need to try and heed is to distance yourself from other negative people. If you spend time with positive people and are bathed in their can-do attitude, it will rub off on you and you will follow suit. It also works the other way, if you spend lots of time surrounded by negative people, listening to problems they refuse to change, their negativity will bring you down just as surely as the former group's positivity will bolster your own.

Make sure you also give thanks for what you have and have achieved, rather than focusing on what you do not have. Count your blessings daily and depending on what you believe, thank your God or the universe for them. Think about the people in your life who make it richer just by being in it, give thanks for a functional, working body – or the bits of it which do work rather than lamenting those which do not – always remember, you could always be in a worse place, but you need to think positive to get into a better one.

From Little Acorns

Often people tell you to, 'go big or go home,' or to, 'not sweat the small stuff.'

Why? It makes no sense, in the often used money making question, 'What would you rather have, a million dollars now or one cent doubled daily for the next month?' The majority of people would go for the instant million whereas, once you figure it out – go on, grab a calculator and have a go – you find you would actually be better off beginning with the smaller amount.

What effect does this have on bodyweight training? Even the smallest thing can have immense impact on your goals.

When you are beginning something, especially something life changing like a new exercise regime, you might see it as a mountain you have to climb to get over and wonder how you will ever get all the way up there.

Take the first step. That is how. If you stand at the bottom of your virtual mountain and just stare up, you will never get there, if you set off on the walk you eventually will. Think about the saying, 'A journey of a thousand miles begins with a single step.' It is the same philosophy, if you are unwilling to take that initial step, you are getting nowhere.

So you do need to sweat the small stuff and you should also ignore all that rubbish about going big or going home. Take a little step first. Then take another and another and soon you will be striding, *sprinting*, towards the top of that rocky hill. You might find a different path to get there, you might even find an easier path, but you will never get there if you do not set off.

Bodyweight training might seem like a mountainous climb to some, others might find it easier. However, if you look at it from the perspective of being at the bottom, it might be daunting. Bodyweight training is *hard*, there is no arguing with that, but it is also *possible*. So do not begin your journey towards the peak of your bodyweight training mountain by setting your sights on the peak, where you have the perfectly sculpted muscular body you want. Begin with small steps, small goals and let the cumulative effect help you to the top of that mountain.

Many people fail at things in life regardless of how many times they try, not because they are not dedicated, or because they are thinking negatively, but simply because their goals are way too big. You can achieve those big goals but not by the end of tomorrow, you will get overwhelmed by the prospect of such massive goals in such a short time, failure is inevitable.

Setting smaller, more achievable goals actually helps you to succeed in your bodyweight training by breaking down the massive mountain into smaller 'mole hills' you can just step over. By setting and then achieving these smaller goals, you will become more confident in your abilities. Your skills – coordination, balance – will increase, your strength will increase too as will your knowledge – not only practical knowledge like how to do the individual exercises but the knowledge you can achieve your smaller goals – leading to your self-belief and momentum.

Momentum in this case is the fact that one small step will lead to another, then another and because you have gained that little bit of knowledge or experience, your steps – or goals – can start to get bigger as a consequence. Start achieving bigger goals and your steps increase again – momentum.

So when my daughter was taking her first steps, she did not think, 'By the time I am five, I will have to be walking to school and running around with my friends.' She did not think of it at all, she just stood up one day in the middle of the room and took a step. Needless to say she then fell back on her butt, yet she got up again and carried on. Obviously this analogy does not relate as fully to your goals, most children learn to walk without thinking about it, but a lesson can be learned from it nevertheless. Small goals, lead to bigger goals and then on to your ultimate goals.

You need to take the small steps to begin to move, stay with small steps to keep up the progress and begin to make habits and use those habits to let you take the bigger steps Needless to say, however, there are little habits you already have which prevent you from taking those bigger steps, over thinking things, doubting yourself and making excuses along with self-doubt make your steps falter and halt.

As with the power of positive thought above, you can tackle these negative habits by taking small steps towards the goal you want to achieve. Change one negative habit into a positive one at a time until the bigger goals are met. Always remember, there are no positive actions you can take which are too small and no negative habits you have should be ignored.

Listen to Your Body

One of the single most important things you can do to aid quick recovery is to listen to what your body is telling you. If you feel sore, tired and notice that your performance is decreasing, you need to take a break altogether or increase the amount of recovery time you have included. If you feel good and strong the day after a hard training session, there is no need to take it slowly. Pay attention to what your body is saying because it will always tell you what it needs and when it needs it.

Chapter 7
Advanced Bodyweight Exercises

Although bodyweight has made a huge comeback, there are still those who believe that it can only get you to a certain stage before you need to move on to something else. Yes, you can do pushups and sit-ups all day long and you will only go so far but, to shake things up a bit, you can make these more difficult to do and push through the plateau you have reached. The following are four of the more advanced bodyweight exercises that anyone who has mastered basic bodyweight can do:

Handstand Push-up

A normal pushup involves you pressing your body horizontally to the ground and pushing up using your chest, hands and arms. A handstand push-up is more like an overhead press with the emphasis on your shoulders instead. As well as that, putting your body into a vertical position means that you are lifting more weight than you would of your feet were on the ground:

- Stand up and face the wall
- Put yourself into a handstand position against the wall
- Engage your glutes, abs and thigh muscles
- Lower your head to the ground, as far as you possibly can
- Push up and repeat

Muscle Up

This is a rare beast of an exercise, one that works the upper body by pulling and pushing, using serious core strength. Those who are not familiar with it may think it is nothing more than a pull-up and dip but it is more than that – so much more that just one requires serious strength:

- Hang from a pull-up bar or rings using a false grip – thumbs should be on top of the bar or ring and the wrist over the top
- Pull yourself right up
- Roll over the bar or rings to transition from a pull-up into a dip

- Pressing your hands down, push your body upwards into the dip
- Lower yourself and repeat

Pistol Squat

One-legged pistol squats are fantastic for building up strength in the lower body as we as improving your flexibility and balance. No equipment is required and this s one of the best single leg squats there is:

- Stand straight and tall on one leg
- Lower yourself to the floor, keeping your foot flat to the ground
- Extend the other leg in front of you, engaging your core muscles and keeping your chest up
- Extend your arms in front of you
- Return to the standing position and repeat

Shrimp Squat

This is a more challenging vision of a single leg squat. Some people will find this easier than the pistol while others will find it harder to do. Instead of holding your leg out in front, the shrimp requires that you hold it behind you:

- Stand up straight

- Bend one knee and grab hold of the ankle behind your back
- Lower yourself until the bended knee is touching the ground
- Stretch your leg out behind you and reach your arm out to the front – this will counterbalance your weight
- Ease back up to a standing position and repeat

To make things even tougher, start from the ground position and push up – it will be much harder because you don't have that downward momentum to help you.

These toughened bodyweight exercises are really just the beginning. There are plenty of variations and changes that you can make to standard bodyweight exercises to make things tougher on yourself, working those muscles harder and pushing yourself that little bit further each time.

Chapter 8
The Best Ab Workouts for Ripped Abs

Ask yourself how many times you have decided against working out your abs because, although you had good intentions of doing it after your training session, you were simply too worn out to even think about it. If you can honestly say that this is you, then I may just have the solution you have been looking for – a bodyweight workout for your abs that you can do anywhere, at any time. You can do this in the comfort of your own home, as soon as you get up in the morning or when you come home from work and it won't take that long to start seeing results. This workout is designed to target all of your abdominal muscles in the best way possible.

Before I get on to the routine, I just want to cover a number of concepts that are vital, concepts that many people don't even know about when it comes to getting your abs on show in all their ripped glory. First, its one thing to work your abdominal muscles but it's quite another to see them. To do that, you have to get rid of some of that body fat covering them. In general, a woman should have approximately 12-13% body fat while a man should be at about 6-8%. How do you get your body fat percentage down?

1. **Following the Correct Nutritional Program**

It doesn't matter how much exercise you do, how many crunches you do in the mornings, your abs will not make an appearance if they are smothered in a layer of fat. A good nutrition program should consist of 40-50% good carbohydrates, 40-35% protein, and 20% good fats.

2. **Following a Proper Training Routine**

That includes bodyweight training and, depending on how experienced you are and what your goals are, you can do as little as three full body workouts in the comfort of your own home or as much as five or six advanced training sessions a week. Some people question the need for bodyweight training when it comes to showing off their abs and the main reason for it is to give you a toned and shapely frame.

Really and truthfully, no matter what you see or read on the TV or internet, aerobics exercise is not enough to tone your abs; it has to be some form of bodyweight training. Bodyweight training also permanently increases your metabolism because of the increase in muscle mass that you gain – don't panic, you won't look like Arnold Schwarzenegger unless you choose to and ladies, you won't anyway because you simply don't have the testosterone levels required.

3. **Do Sufficient Cardiovascular Exercise**

The best way to burn off extra calories is to perform cardiovascular exercise first thing in the morning on an empty stomach or as soon as you have finished your exercise session. This in turn will help to burn off more fat. You don't need to overdo it because too much cardio will burn your muscles out and will also lower your metabolism, not what you are looking to do. Aim for between three and five sessions, each one about half an hour, per week will be sufficient.

4. **Do the Right Abdominal Exercises to Shape your Abs**

This is the crux of this chapter and what it's all about. The following exercise plan is perfect for getting those abs in shape, ready to be shown off:

Exercise Number 1 – Crunches

- Lie on the floor with your back flat
- Your legs should be bent at the knees and your hands crossed over your chest

- Start by raising up your torso and shoulders as far as you can, using a curling motion – try not to raise your back too much as you exhale
- Keeping tension in your abdominal muscles, inhale and return to your starting position

Try to avoid rocking backwards and forwards keep full control throughout the entire movement. You can place a rolled towel under your spine curvature – this will stretch your abdominal wall to its fullest, giving you a fuller range of motion

Exercise Number 2 – Bicycle Crunches

- Lie on the floor with your back flat on the floor and place your hands to the sides of your head
- Lift your shoulders up as if you were doing a standard crunch and raise your knees so they are perpendicular to the floor and your lower legs parallel to the floor – this is your start position
- Now perform a slow cycle pedaling motion – kick forward with the right log, bringing the left knee in. At the same time, take your right elbow over to the left knee, crunching sideways as you exhale
- Go back to your start position as you inhale and crunch to the opposite side

- Continue alternating until you have carried out the number of repetitions you have set.

Try to avoid straining your neck and take this one slow and steady – sloppy and fast work will result in an injury

Exercise Number 3 – Lying Leg Raises

- Lie flat on the floor with your legs out in front of you
- Put your hands, palms down, flat on the floor beside you as support
- Flex your abs and raise your legs up, exhaling as you do, until they are perpendicular to the floor
- Keeping your abs under tension, lower your legs back down to your starting position but stop when they are about an inch off the floor as you breath in

Try to avoid letting your legs drop to the floor, as this will negate any benefit of the exercise

Exercise Number 4 – Modified V-Ups

- Sit on the floor or chair and use your hands for support as you extend your legs out in front

- Bring your legs as far up as they will go while, at the same time, moving your torso towards them as you inhale
- Return to your start position while exhaling and repeat until your set is finished
- Try to avoid dropping your legs and keep full control of your body

Exercise Number 5 – Knee-Ins

- Sit on the edge of a chair or on the floor and extend your legs out in front of you. Keep your hands on the floor or holding the chair for support
- Hold your knees together and pull them in to your chest as your breathe out, until you can't go any further
- Hold the tension in your abs and return to your starting position as your breathe in
- Repeat until all reps have been completed

Avoid fast movements and keep full control of your body throughout the exercise

Bodyweight Ripped Abs Program

Your goal here is to boost your metabolism and shape up those abdominal muscles. Complete the following program three times per week with a rest day in between. The best time is first thing in the morning; continue for 6 weeks.

EXERCISE	SETS	REPS	TARGET MUSCLES	SECONDARY TARGETS
Crunches	3	10-21	Upper abs	Obliques, lower abs
Bicycle Crunches	3	10-21	Full abdominal wall	None
Lying Leg Raises	3	10-21	Lower abs	Obliques, upper abs
Modified V-Ups	3	10-21	Lower abs, Upper abs	Obliques
Knee-Ins	3	10-21	Lower abs	Obliques, upper abs

Perform this program in a circuit training fashion. For weeks one and two, rest for 30 seconds between each exercise set. Rest for two minutes before you start the circuit again. For weeks three and four, do not rest between each exercise and only for 1 minute between circuits. For the final two weeks, try to do all three sets without any rest between

Conclusion

Strength building is a process that requires not just time and patience, but also hard work and dedication. Without a combination of the mentioned elements, you simply cannot hope to achieve the desired results of your work out regimes. Everyone dreams of getting the perfect body but seldom go through with the tedious and often laborious procedure to get one.

Words and advice will only go so far to push you into working out. Get up and hit the treadmill. Sitting around won't make you a healthy person. Adopt a balanced diet to supplement your efforts. Eat meat, green leafy vegetables, pulses, and fish and drink as much water as possible as when you sweat it out in the gym, you lose a lot of water from your body.

Thank you for downloading this eBook. I hope you won't stop at that and go ahead to follow through with the laid down ways to get yourself that alluring body you have always wanted.

Made in the USA
Middletown, DE
02 February 2018